Green Line **4**

Vokabellernheft

von
Martina Nolte-Bohres

herausgegeben von
Harald Weisshaar

Ernst Klett Verlag
Stuttgart · Leipzig

Vorwort

Liebe Schülerin, lieber Schüler,

in den vergangenen drei Schuljahren hast du eine ganze Menge Vokabeln gelernt und dir so schon einen beachtlichen englischen Wortschatz angeeignet. Das Green Line 4 Vokabellernheft unterstützt dich dabei, diesen im 8. Schuljahr noch zu erweitern. Du kannst mit dem Vokabellernheft den gesamten Lernwortschatz wiederholen und üben, und das nicht nur zu Hause, sondern auch unterwegs, denn es passt in deine Hosentasche. Durch die Gliederung der Vokabeln nach den Buchteilen verlierst du nie den Überblick darüber, welche Wörter du schon kannst und welche du dir noch einmal anschauen musst. Tipps zum Vokabellernen findest du zu Beginn jeder Unit.

Zusätzlich zum Wortschatz bietet dir dein Vokabellernheft auch abwechslungsreiche Übungen, in denen du die gelernten Wörter direkt nach jedem Abschnitt anwendest. Dies hilft dir dabei, die Vokabeln gut zu behalten, und bereitet dich gleichzeitig auf Tests vor. Am Ende jeder Unit bzw. Text smart gibt es eine Übung zur Selbstkontrolle (Check on your …), mit der du herausfinden kannst, wie fit du in einem bestimmten Thema bist.

Markiere beim Lernen alle Wörter und Wendungen, die du dir nicht so gut merken kannst, mit einem Bleistift. Wiederhole sie dann in regelmäßigen Abständen.

Mit den Lösungen auf den Seiten 87 bis 96 überprüfst du dich schließlich selbst.

Viel Spaß und Erfolg mit deinem Vokabellernheft!

Dein Green Line Team

Englische Laute

Mitlaute (Konsonanten)

[b]	**b**ed	[p]	**p**icture
[d]	**d**ay	[r]	**r**ed
[ð]	**th**e	[s]	**s**ix
[f]	**f**amily	[ʃ]	**sh**e
[g]	**g**o	[t]	**t**en
[ŋ]	morni**ng**	[tʃ]	**ch**air
[h]	**h**ouse	[v]	**v**ideo
[j]	**y**ou	[w]	**w**e, **o**ne
[k]	**c**an, mil**k**	[z]	ea**s**y
[l]	**l**etter	[ʒ]	revi**si**on
[m]	**m**an	[dʒ]	pa**ge**
[n]	**n**o	[θ]	**th**ank you

Selbstlaute (Vokale)

[ɑː]	c**a**r	[i]	happ**y**
[æ]	**a**pple	[iː]	t**ea**cher
[e]	p**e**n	[ɒ]	d**o**g
[ə]	**a**gain	[ɔː]	b**a**ll
[ɜː]	g**ir**l	[ʊ]	b**oo**k
[ʌ]	b**u**t	[u]	J**a**nuary
[ɪ]	**i**t	[uː]	t**oo**, tw**o**

Doppellaute

[aɪ]	**I**, m**y**	[ɪə]	h**ere**, **i**dea
[aʊ]	n**ow**, m**ou**se	[əʊ]	hell**o**
[eɪ]	n**a**me, th**ey**	[ɔɪ]	b**oy**
[eə]	th**ere**, p**air**	[ʊə]	s**ure**

[ː] der vorangehende Laut ist lang, z. B. *you* [juː]
[‿] der Bindebogen zeigt, dass zwei Wörter in der Aussprache verbunden werden
['] die folgende Silbe trägt den Hauptakzent
[ˌ] die folgende Silbe trägt den Nebenakzent

AC1

Across cultures 1 The USA: Country of contrasts

> **Tip**
>
> Welcome back! Du kommst sicher gut erholt aus den Sommerferien. Vielleicht hast du sogar im Urlaub ab und zu Englisch gesprochen? Um Schritt für Schritt wieder ins Englischlernen einzusteigen, kannst du jeden Tag ein paar zufällig ausgewählte Vokabeln wiederholen: Zieh einfach einige Karten aus deiner Kartei oder schließ die Augen und tippe mit dem Finger auf die Vokabellisten im Heft oder Buch.

contrast ['kɒntrɑːst]	Kontrast; Unterschied; Gegensatz
the US (= the United States) [ðə juːˈes]	die USA (= die Vereinigten Staaten)
urban ['ɜːbn]	städtisch; Stadt-
endless ['endləs]	endlos
sparse [spɑːs]	dünn; spärlich
populated ['pɒpjəleɪtɪd]	bevölkert; besiedelt
rural ['rʊərl]	ländlich
single ['sɪŋgl]	einzeln; einzig; alleinstehend
tractor ['træktə]	Traktor
desert ['dezət]	Wüste
(the) Southwest [ˌsaʊθˈwest]	(der) Südwesten; im Südwesten; südwestlich
temperature ['temprətʃə]	Temperatur
degree Fahrenheit (°F) ['færnhaɪt]	Grad Fahrenheit
cactus ['kæktəs]	Kaktus
cool [kuːl]	kühl
zone [zəʊn]	Zone
immigrant ['ɪmɪgrənt]	Immigrant/-in; Einwanderer/-in

AC 1

European [ˌjʊərəˈpiːən]	Europäer/-in; europäisch; aus Europa
cultural [ˈkʌltʃrl]	kulturell
redwood (tree) [ˈredwʊd ˌtriː]	Mammutbaum
foot [fʊt], **feet** [fiːt] *(pl)*	Fuß *(Längenmaß: 30,48 cm)*
skyscraper [ˈskaɪskreɪpə]	Wolkenkratzer
state [steɪt]	Staat; Bundesstaat; Land
to **fly** [flaɪ], **flew** [fluː], **flown** [fləʊn]	hissen
a (day/week/year) [ə ˈdeɪ/wiːk/jɪə]	pro (Tag/Woche/Jahr)
population [ˌpɒpjəˈleɪʃn]	Bevölkerung; Population
billionaire [ˈbɪliəneə]	Milliardär/-in
scenery [ˈsiːnri]	Landschaft
simply [ˈsɪmpli]	einfach nur
dense [dens]	dicht
in the country [ˌɪn ðə ˈkʌntri]	auf dem Land
mountainous [ˈmaʊntɪnəs]	bergig
flat [flæt]	flach; platt
gigantic [dʒaɪˈgæntɪk]	gigantisch; riesig
wealthy [ˈwelθi]	wohlhabend; reich
wasteful [ˈweɪstfl]	verschwenderisch
luxury [ˈlʌkʃri]	Luxus
to **represent** [ˌreprɪˈzent]	repräsentieren; darstellen; stehen für
to **symbolize** *(AE)* [ˈsɪmbəlaɪz]	symbolisieren
harsh [hɑːʃ]	rau; hart
extreme [ɪkˈstriːm]	extrem; radikal
standard of living [ˌstændəd əv ˈlɪvɪŋ]	Lebensstandard
to **become friends** [bɪˌkʌm ˈfrendz]	sich anfreunden; Freundschaft schließen

vacation *(AE)* [vəˈkeɪʃn]	Ferien; Urlaub
dude *(coll)* [duːd]	Mann; Alter *(ugs.)*
awesome [ˈɔːsəm]	super; spitze
US [juːˈes]	US-amerikanisch
to **have no clue** [ˌhæv nəʊ ˈkluː]	keine Ahnung haben
route planner [ˈruːt ˌplænə]	Routenplaner
Brit [brɪt]	Brite/Britin *(ugs.)*
colonist [ˈkɒlənɪst]	Siedler/-in; Kolonist/-in
corn [kɔːn]	Korn; Mais; Getreide
wheat [wiːt]	Weizen
to **ride** [raɪd], **rode** [rəʊd], **ridden** [ˈrɪdn]	fahren; reiten
epic [ˈepɪk]	episch; *hier:* geil
massive [ˈmæsɪv]	riesig; massiv; *hier:* super
complete [kəmˈpliːt]	vollständig; komplett; völlig

1 Contrasts in the US

Put in the correct opposites.

1. In _____ areas, you have a huge choice of shops, theatres or restaurants, but you find fewer open spaces than in _____ areas.

2. There are many _____ or even rich people in the US – 10 million millionaires is a really large number! But many Americans are _____ : They don't have enough money although they have two jobs or more.

AC1

3. Cities are _____ populated. When people from New York come to the _____ populated Midwest, they often feel like they're in a different world.

Word groups: Rural or urban?

Write the words or phrases in the correct part of the grid.

crowded   parks   endless   corn   taxi   scenery
wheat   skyscraper   redwood tree   Broadway plays
cactus   tractor   densely populated   noisy

In the city	In the country

AC 1

3 That's the US!

Put in the correct adjectives.

| extreme | awesome | cultural | rural | European | harsh |

Tristan: Many _____ immigrants came to the US in the 19th and 20th centuries. My family came from London.

Callum: So you're a Brit! Maybe there aren't that many _____ differences between you and me …

Tristan: No, dude! We're going to have an _____ time together, I'm sure.

Callum: I hope it'll be warmer in California than in London.

Tristan: I bet it will. Sometimes we have really _____ temperatures here. Too hot, even for me!

Callum: But there are also areas in the US which have a really _____ climate …

Tristan: But you aren't going to Alaska, are you?! It's much too _____ anyway, at least for me!

Unit 1 Kids in America

> **Tip**
>
> Bei Wörtern wie *exaggerated* kannst du dir vielleicht nicht sofort ihre Schreibung genau merken. In solchen Fällen hilft es, sie mehrmals hintereinander aufzuschreiben und die Buchstabenfolge laut aufzusagen.

kid [kɪd]	Jugendliche/-r; Kind

Introduction

impression [ɪmˈpreʃn]	Impression; Eindruck
orientation [ˌɔːriənˈteɪʃn]	Orientierung; Orientierungs-
to **give a talk** [ˌgɪv ə ˈtɔːk]	einen Vortrag halten
suburb [ˈsʌbɜːb]	Vorort
suburban [səˈbɜːbn]	Vorstadt-
front yard *(AE)* [ˌfrʌnt ˈjɑːd]	Vorgarten
shopping mall [ˈʃɒpɪŋ ˌmɔːl]	Einkaufszentrum
middle school *(AE)* [ˈmɪdl ˌskuːl]	Mittelschule *(weiterführende Schule in den USA, Mittelstufe)*
high school *(AE)* [ˈhaɪ ˌskuːl]	High School *(weiterführende Schule in den USA, Oberstufe)*
hallway [ˈhɔːlweɪ]	Flur; Diele; Korridor
hall pass [ˈhɔːl pɑːs]	*Erlaubnis, sich während des Unterrichts auf dem Flur aufzuhalten*
dress code [ˈdres ˌkəʊd]	Kleiderordnung; Bekleidungsvorschriften
restroom *(AE)* [ˈrestrʊm]	Toilette

1

1 Word friends: American everyday life

Make pairs of two words and write them down.

school   code
mall   front   pass
middle   school
hall   high   yard
shopping   dress

1. _____
2. _____
3. _____
4. _____
5. _____
6. _____

2 What word?

Read the words in the phonetic alphabet and write them down. The grid on page 3 will help you.

1. [ɪmˈpreʃn]

   _____

2. [ˈhɔːlweɪ]

   _____

3. [ˈrestrʊm]

   _____

4. [ˈsʌbɜːb]

   _____

Station 1: Living here isn't bad

movie *(AE)* [ˈmuːvi]	Film
walk-in closet [ˌwɔːkɪn ˈklɒzɪt]	begehbarer Kleiderschrank
to **be around** [ˌbi: əˈraʊnd]	da sein; zusammen sein mit
not until [ˌnɒt ənˈtɪl]	nicht vor; erst um/im
store *(AE)* [stɔː]	Laden; Geschäft
drive [draɪv]	Fahrt; Anfahrt; Autofahrt
along for the ride [əˌlɒŋ fə ðə ˈraɪd]	mit dabei
ride [raɪd]	Fahrt; Ritt
curfew [ˈkɜːfjuː]	Sperrstunde; Ausgangssperre
to **meet up** [ˌmiːt ˈʌp]	sich treffen
downtown *(AE)* [ˌdaʊnˈtaʊn]	im Stadtzentrum
to **get used to sth** [ˌget ˈjuːzd tə]	sich an etw. gewöhnen
floor [flɔː]	Stockwerk
elevator *(AE)* [ˈelɪveɪtə]	Aufzug; Lift
luckily [ˈlʌkɪli]	glücklicherweise
movie theater *(AE)* [ˈmuːvi ˌθɪətə]	Kino
soccer *(AE)* [ˈsɒkə]	Fußball
I'm afraid … [ˌaɪm əˈfreɪd]	Leider …
to **keep in touch** [ˌkiːp ɪn ˈtʌtʃ]	in Kontakt bleiben
to **keep** [kiːp], **kept** [kept], **kept** [kept]	*hier:* weiter tun; immer wieder tun
no wonder [ˌnəʊ ˈwʌndə]	kein Wunder
Pilgrim [ˈpɪlgrɪm]	Pilger/-in
to **practice a religion** [ˌpræktɪs ə rɪˈlɪdʒn]	eine Religion ausüben
survivor [səˈvaɪvə]	Überlebende/-r
Native American [ˌneɪtɪv əˈmerɪkən]	Ureinwohner/-in Amerikas; Indianer/-in; indianisch

1

harvest [ˈhɑːvɪst]	Ernte
to **give thanks** [ˌɡɪv ˈθæŋks]	danken
Indian [ˈɪndiən]	Indianer/-in; indianisch
menu [ˈmenjuː]	Speisekarte
dish [dɪʃ]	Gericht; Speise
instead of [ɪnˈsted ˌəv]	statt; anstatt; an Stelle von
social media [ˌsəʊʃl ˈmiːdiə]	soziale Netzwerke
to **mind** [maɪnd]	etwas dagegen haben; einem etwas ausmachen
in the middle of nowhere [ɪn ðə ˌmɪdl əv ˈnəʊweə]	mitten im Nirgendwo
to **find one's way around** [ˌfaɪnd wʌnz ˌweɪ əˈraʊnd]	sich zurechtfinden
to **be tired of** [bi ˈtaɪəd ˌəv]	es müde sein (zu); es leid sein (zu); es satt haben (zu)
likes *(pl)* [laɪks]	Vorlieben
dislikes *(pl)* [dɪsˈlaɪks]	Abneigungen
to **unpack** [ʌnˈpæk]	auspacken
to **dislike** [dɪsˈlaɪk]	nicht mögen
to **dream** [driːm], **dreamt** [dremt], **dreamt** [dremt]	träumen
to **be crazy about** [bi ˈkreɪzi ˌəbaʊt]	verrückt sein nach; abfahren auf
insecure [ˌɪnsɪˈkjʊə]	unsicher
foreground [ˈfɔːɡraʊnd]	Vordergrund

3 Say it in American English!

Write down the American English words for the British English ones.

1. football

   _____

2. film

   _____

3. shop

   _____

4. cinema

   _____

4 My new life in the US

Put the correct words in Matt's e-mail to his grandma.

Dear Grandma,

I really like Pittsburgh. We live in an apartment close to ☐☐☐☐☐☐`n`☐, on the 22nd (!) ☐`l`☐☐☐, so I spend a lot of time in the ☐☐☐`a`☐☐☐☐. `L`☐☐☐☐☐☐☐, there are shops and cafés super close to where I live.

I have to stop now, I'm ☐☐☐☐☐☐☐.

My friends are waiting for me in front of the ☐`o`☐☐☐ ☐☐☐☐☐☐☐☐.

Let's ☐☐`e`☐ ☐☐ ☐☐☐☐☐

by e-mail!

Yours, Matt

5 Sophie calls Matt

Complete what Sophie says with the correct phrases. They're all new phrases in Station 1.

Hi Matt! How are you? I'm at my aunt and uncle's house – it's

_____. I'm so bored! At least it's

easy to _____ my _____

because there aren't many streets, so it's hard to get lost!

I _____ driving two hours to the next

mall. Luckily, we're moving to Pittsburgh soon – I'd never

_____ living in the country! There's only one

thing I _____ : Tom's Café. They have the

best ice cream in the world! _____ I had to

wait for 20 minutes yesterday to get my "chocolate surprise"!

6 Odd word out

Cross out the word that doesn't fit.

1. harvest | wheat | dish | curfew
2. keep in touch | meet up | give thanks | hang out with
3. trip | floor | drive | ride
4. foreground | elevator | stairs | floor
5. be tired of | dislike | be crazy about | hate

Station 2: That's the worst thing to do!

committee [kəˈmɪti]	Komitee; Ausschuss
8th-grader *(AE)* [ˈeɪtθˌgreɪdə]	Achtklässler/-in
period *(AE)* [ˈpɪəriəd]	Stunde; Unterrichtsstunde
geek [giːk]	Außenseiter/-in
What a … [ˈwɒt ə]	Was für ein/-e …
shopper [ˈʃɒpə]	Käufer/-in
child labor *(AE)* [ˌtʃaɪld ˈleɪbə]	Kinderarbeit
sweatshop [ˈswetʃɒp]	Ausbeuterbetrieb
to **demonstrate** [ˈdemənstreɪt]	demonstrieren
right [raɪt]	Recht
whether [ˈweðə]	ob
to **prefer** [prɪˈfɜː]	vorziehen
to **control** [kənˈtrəʊl]	kontrollieren; steuern
might [maɪt]	könnte/-n (vielleicht)
to **argue** [ˈɑːgjuː]	argumentieren; streiten
to **clean out** [ˌkliːn ˈaʊt]	ausräumen; entrümpeln
clothing drive [ˈkləʊðɪŋ ˌdraɪv]	Kleidersammlung
homeless shelter [ˈhəʊmləs ˌʃeltə]	Obdachlosenunterkunft
homeless [ˈhəʊmləs]	obdachlos
to **wish** [wɪʃ]	(sich) wünschen
to **donate** [dəˈneɪt]	spenden; stiften
benefit [ˈbenɪfɪt]	Vorteil; Nutzen; Unterstützung
pound [paʊnd]	Pfund *(Maßeinheit)*
item [ˈaɪtəm]	Gegenstand; Objekt
drop-off [ˈdrɒpɒf]	Abgabe

7 Matt's dilemma

Put in the missing words. The words in brackets are definitions that will help you.

1. In second _____ **(AE word for 'lesson')**, Matt is looking at different layouts with two of the most popular _____ **(students in the 8th year of school)**, Scott and Eva.

2. Scott and Eva think that Henry and Tyler are _____ **(persons who are different from most of the others)** because they demonstrate against _____ **(adults' work done by children)**.

3. Eva says that Henry and Tyler shout at the _____ **(people who buy something)** in the mall and adds that they want her and the others to write about children's _____ **(what people are allowed to do or say)** in the yearbook. But she _____ **(like better)** to write about fun things.

Story: Nightmare at the mall!

nightmare [ˈnaɪtmeə]	Alptraum
believable [bɪˈliːvəbl]	glaubwürdig
exaggerated [ɪgˈzædʒreɪtɪd]	übertrieben
unrealistic [ˌʌnrɪəˈlɪstɪk]	unrealistisch
coincidence [kəʊˈɪnsɪdns]	Zufall
to **open** [ˈəʊpn]	eröffnen
to **sign** [saɪn]	unterschreiben; unterzeichnen
amazed [əˈmeɪzd]	erstaunt; verblüfft
scared [skeəd]	verängstigt; ängstlich
right [raɪt]	direkt
cheer [tʃɪə]	Jubel; Hurraruf
dizzy [ˈdɪzi]	schwindelig
down [daʊn]	nieder
to **escape (from)** [ɪˈskeɪp frəm]	fliehen; entfliehen; flüchten; entkommen
protester [ˈprəʊtestə]	Protestierende/-r; Demonstrant/-in
to **touch** [tʌtʃ]	berühren; antippen
troublemaker [ˈtrʌblmeɪkə]	Unruhestifter/-in
to **leave sb alone** [ˌliːv əˈləʊn]	jmdn. in Ruhe lassen
obvious [ˈɒbviəs]	offensichtlich
twice [twaɪs]	zweimal
mess [mes]	Unordnung; Durcheinander; Schweinerei
to **mix** [mɪks]	zusammenpassen

8 Adjectives for people and things

Write the adjectives in the correct part of the grid.

obvious   amazed   dizzy   believable   scared   unrealistic   exaggerated   confident

People can be ...	Things can be ...

9 Definitions

Put in the correct words.

1. Something that's easy to see or understand is

   _____.

2. A _____ is a scary dream.

3. If you run away from something, you

   _____ from it.

4. If you do something two times, you do it

   _____.

Word friends

Draw lines to match the verbs and nouns that are often used together.

1. open
2. sign
3. escape from
4. touch
5. tidy up

a) a mess
b) the ground
c) a store
d) a T-shirt or book
e) a crowd

Jumbled sentences

Find the right word order and make sentences.

1. to | I'm | stay | you | right | going | to | next

___

2. and | Lena | feel | to | dizzy | started | sick

___

3. prison | could | she | spending | imagine | night | in | easily | a

___

___

4. face | around | came | she | to | with | face | Matt | turned | and

___

Action USA! Go on, text her!

Go on! [ˌgəʊ ˈɒn]	Los!
attractive [əˈtræktɪv]	attraktiv
boyfriend [ˈbɔɪfrend]	Freund *(in einer Paarbeziehung)*
attitude [ˈætɪtjuːd]	Haltung; Einstellung
to overdo [əʊvəˈduː], **overdid** [əʊvəˈdɪd], **overdone** [əʊvəˈdʌn]	übertreiben; zu weit gehen
date [deɪt]	Verabredung; Date

Skills: How to write in the appropriate style

content [ˈkɒntent]	Inhalt
toothpaste [ˈtuːθpeɪst]	Zahnpasta
ironic [ˌaɪˈrɒnɪk]	ironisch
informative [ɪnˈfɔːmətɪv]	informativ
natural [ˈnætʃrl]	natürlich; Natur-
individual [ˌɪndɪˈvɪdʒuəl]	Einzelperson; Einzelne/-r; Individuum
pose [pəʊz]	Pose; Haltung
season [ˈsiːzn]	Saison; Jahreszeit
championship [ˈtʃæmpiənʃɪp]	Meisterschaft

Unit task: An American-style yearbook

double [ˈdʌbl]	Doppel-; zweimal
concert [ˈkɒnsət]	Konzert

12 Opposites

Find the opposite of each word.

1. group _____

2. girlfriend _____

3. background ➘ _____

4. to like ➘ _____

3 Yearbook texts

Put in the correct words.

| poses | informative | content | overdo | ironic |

A yearbook is divided into different sections, and each section

has its own typical _____ and language tone.

In 'Clubs and Sports', the style is _____ , in

'Student Superlatives' you can find _____

comments on funny _____ for photos too.

But students shouldn't _____ it – they might

hurt somebody's feelings.

4 Check on your … AE vocabulary

Make a list of the American English words you've learned in Unit 1.

_____

_____

_____

_____

_____

Text smart 1 Advertisements

> **Tip**
>
> Du kannst dein Englisch super üben, indem du immer mal wieder einen englischen Text liest. Such doch im Internet nach Artikeln aus englischsprachigen Zeitungen oder Zeitschriften zu einem Thema, das dich interessiert. Oder du liest eine Kurzgeschichte auf Englisch!

ad(vertisement) [əd'vɜːtɪsmənt]	Anzeige; Werbespot
product ['prɒdʌkt]	Produkt; Erzeugnis
just about anywhere [ˌdʒʌst əˌbaʊt 'eniweə]	praktisch überall
advertiser ['ædvətaɪzə]	Werbefachmann/-frau
to **win sb over** [ˌwɪn ˈəʊvə]	jmdn. für sich gewinnen; jmdn. überzeugen

Introduction

brand [brænd]	Marke
immediately [ɪ'miːdiətli]	sofort; gleich
to **give away** [ˌgɪv ə'weɪ]	verteilen; verschenken
sample ['sɑːmpl]	Probe; Muster
chocolate bar ['tʃɒklət ˌbɑː]	Schokoriegel
to **fall for** ['fɔːl fə]	hereinfallen auf
hair [heə]	Haar; Haare
to **advertise** ['ædvətaɪz]	Werbung machen; werben; anpreisen; inserieren
receptive [rɪ'septɪv]	empfänglich
temptation [temp'teɪʃn]	Versuchung
sceptical ['skeptɪkl]	skeptisch
advertising *(no pl)* ['ædvətaɪzɪŋ]	Werbung; Reklame

TS 1

1 Phrasal verbs

a) *Find the correct prepositions for the verbs and write down the phrasal verbs. Use each preposition only once. The phrasal verbs are all new in* Green Line 4.

meet   give   rely   on   out   up
win   fall   clean   over   away   for

1. _____   4. _____

2. _____   5. _____

3. _____   6. _____

b) *Complete the text with the phrasal verbs from a).*

Advertisers try to _____ customers

_____ in different ways.

They _____ free samples of a

product, for example, and hope that people will

_____ this trick. Or customers are told in

ads that they should really _____ their

closets in spring and then _____ with

their friends in the mall to buy new outfits for the summer.

They _____ people wanting to be cool

and modern!

TS 1

Station: Did you see that new ad?

to **spice up** [ˌspaɪsˈʌp]	aufpeppen
highly [ˈhaɪli]	höchst-
brand-new [ˌbrændˈnjuː]	brandneu
available [əˈveɪləbl]	erhältlich; verfügbar
glamorous [ˈglæmrəs]	glamourös
lovely [ˈlʌvli]	schön; hübsch
nerd [nɜːd]	Nerd *(Person, die intelligent, aber sozial unbeholfen ist)*
target [ˈtɑːgɪt]	Ziel; Ziel-
eye-catcher [ˈaɪkætʃə]	Blickfang; Hingucker
visual [ˈvɪʒuəl]	Bild
ad copy [ˈæd ˌkɒpi]	Werbetext
image [ˈɪmɪdʒ]	Bild; Abbildung
billboard [ˈbɪlbɔːd]	Plakatwand
approach [əˈprəʊtʃ]	Herangehensweise; Vorgehensweise; Ansatz; Annäherung
truckload [ˈtrʌkləʊd]	Lastwagenladung
arrival [əˈraɪvl]	Ankommende/-r; Neuzugang
to **settle for less** [ˌsetl fə ˈles]	sich mit weniger zufrieden geben
effective [ɪˈfektɪv]	effektiv; wirkungsvoll
to **attract** [əˈtrækt]	anziehen
fabulous [ˈfæbjələs]	sagenhaft; fantastisch
effectiveness [ɪˈfektɪvnəs]	Effektivität; Wirksamkeit

Options

trash *(AE)* [træʃ]	Abfall; Müll
ugly [ˈʌgli]	hässlich

TS 1

2 Word search: Advertising

Find eight advertising words (→, ↓ or ↗) and complete the sentences with three of them.

X	G	N	A	D	C	O	P	Y	A
U	M	L	N	J	O	P	A	P	D
Y	S	A	M	P	L	E	L	R	V
Y	R	N	B	X	K	C	T	O	E
B	I	L	L	B	O	A	R	D	R
S	V	Z	I	R	W	Q	J	U	T
V	I	S	U	A	L	P	K	C	I
R	Z	U	T	E	W	B	S	T	S
I	M	A	G	E	N	H	D	G	E

1. Hey, look at that _____ next to the bus stop. That chocolate bar looks so nice!

2. I was given a free _____ of it at the supermarket yesterday. I really loved it …

3. I've never heard of the _____ before – maybe it's new in the US.

25

TS 1

3 Verb into noun

Find the nouns that belong to the same word family as the verbs.

1. produce ➚ _____ _____

2. tempt ➚ _____

3. wish ➚ _____

4. advertise ➚ _____ _____

   _____

5. arrive ➚ _____

6. survive ➚ _____

4 Check on your ... adjectives

Make a list of adjectives that are useful for writing ads.

_____

_____

_____

_____

_____

_____

_____

_____

/ AC 2

Across cultures 2 School life – dos and don'ts

> **Tip**
>
> Lerne deine Vokabeln ab und zu zusammen mit deinen Freunden. So könnt ihr euch gegenseitig abfragen oder auch Tipps geben, wie ihr euch schwierige Wörter am besten merkt. Das hilft euch nicht nur dabei, die Wörter gut zu können, sondern macht auch Spaß!

corridor [ˈkɒrɪdɔː]	Gang; Flur; Korridor
gym(nasium) [dʒɪm; dʒɪmˈneɪziəm]	Turnhalle
lab(oratory) [læb; ləˈbɒrətri]	Labor
cell phone *(AE)* [ˈselfəʊn]	Mobiltelefon; Handy
to **skip** [skɪp]	auslassen; schwänzen
to **cheat** [tʃiːt]	mogeln; betrügen
to **get caught** [ˌget ˈkɔːt]	erwischt werden; ertappt werden
principal *(AE)* [ˈprɪnsɪpl]	Schulleiter/-in
to **be suspended** [bi səˈspendɪd]	suspendiert werden; zeitweilig vom Unterricht ausgeschlossen werden
detention [dɪˈtenʃn]	Nachsitzen; Haft; Verhaftung
lunchtime [ˈlʌnʃtaɪm]	Mittagszeit; Mittagspause
to **complete** [kəmˈpliːt]	fertigstellen; vervollständigen; vollenden
consequence [ˈkɒnsɪkwəns]	Konsequenz; Folge
otherwise [ˈʌðəwaɪz]	sonst
to **stand in line** *(AE)* [ˌstænd ɪn ˈlaɪn]	anstehen; Schlange stehen; (sich) anstellen
to **switch off** [ˌswɪtʃ ˈɒf]	ausschalten
to **be about to do sth** [bi əˈbaʊt tə]	im Begriff sein, etw. zu tun

AC 2

to **get into trouble** [ˌget ˌɪntə ˈtrʌbl]	in Schwierigkeiten geraten
so (that) [ˌsəʊ ˈðæt]	damit; so dass
cheat sheet [ˈtʃiːt ʃiːt]	Spickzettel
You'd better ... (= You had better) [ˈjuːd ˌbetə]	Du solltest lieber ...
If I were you ... [ˌɪf aɪ wɜː ˈjuː]	Wenn ich du wäre ...
No risk, no fun! [nəʊ ˌrɪsk nəʊ ˈfʌn]	Wer nicht wagt, der nicht gewinnt.
mad [mæd]	wütend
I can't see the point of ... [aɪ ˌkɑːnt siː ðə ˈpɔɪnt ˌəv]	Ich sehe keinen Sinn darin ...
waste [weɪst]	Verschwendung

1 Talking in English

Write down what you could say in the situations described. Use phrases that are new in Across cultures 2.

1. Your younger brother is listening to music instead of doing his homework.

   _____

2. Your best friend got a bad mark in a test and doesn't know how to tell his / her parents. He / She asks what you would do.

   _____

   _____

3. A classmate has said nasty things about you. Your friends think you should talk to him / her, but you think that's useless.

   _____

2 A crossword: School words

Put in the correct words and find the solution.

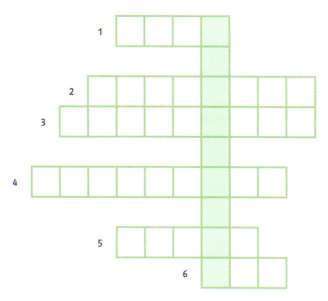

1. If you … a class, you get into trouble.

2. American students aren't allowed to be in the … without a hall pass.

3. If you break a rule several times, you can be … .

4. Students who forget to do their homework very often might get … .

5. If you … on a test, you'll probably get a bad mark.

6. In Science lessons, students often work in the … .

Solution:

A _____ is the "boss" of an American school.

Unit 2 City of dreams: New York

> **Tip**
>
> Du kannst deinen Wortschatz ganz einfach erweitern:
> Sieh dir z. B. deinen Lieblingsfilm auf Englisch an.
> So lernst du Redewendungen für Unterhaltungen!
> Je öfter du Filme auf Englisch anschaust, umso besser
> wirst du die Schauspieler verstehen.

Introduction

intersection [ˌɪntəˈsekʃn]	Kreuzung
district [ˈdɪstrɪkt]	Distrikt; Bezirk
lung [lʌŋ]	Lunge
a pocketful of [ə ˈpɒkɪtfl əv]	Unmengen von/an
gonna (= going to) *(coll)* [ˈgɒnə]	wird/werden
to **make it** [ˈmeɪk ɪt]	es schaffen
by any means [baɪ enɪ ˈmiːnz]	mit allen Mitteln
to **inspire** [ɪnˈspaɪə]	inspirieren; anregen
melting pot [ˈmeltɪŋ ˌpɒt]	Schmelztiegel
jungle [ˈdʒʌŋgl]	Dschungel

1 Word friends: New York

Find the missing words in the noun pairs and write them down.

1. _____ pot

2. concrete _____

3. theater _____

2 Definitions

Put in the correct words.

1. An _____ is a place where two or more roads meet.

2. If you want to say 'a lot of', you can also say '_____'.

3. A person or an event _____ you if it gives you the idea for something, e.g. for a song.

4. A _____ is a place where people from different origins come together to live and form a new culture.

5. A _____ is a forest with a very hot climate.

Station 1: Saving the best for last

to **save the best for last** [ˌseɪv ðə ˌbest fə ˈlɑːst]	sich das Beste bis zum Schluss aufheben
to **take the day off** [ˌteɪk ðə ˌdeɪ ˈɒf]	sich den Tag freinehmen
diner *(AE)* [ˈdaɪnə]	einfaches Restaurant mit Theke und Tischen
conference [ˈkɒnfrns]	Konferenz; Tagung
guidebook [ˈgaɪdbʊk]	Reiseführer
to **gasp** [gɑːsp]	tief Luft holen; keuchen
classical [ˈklæsɪkl]	klassisch
bank [bæŋk]	Bank
sculpture [ˈskʌlptʃə]	Skulptur
since [sɪns]	da
naked [ˈneɪkɪd]	nackt
for free [fə ˈfriː]	umsonst; kostenlos
on a shoestring [ˌɒn ə ˈʃuːstrɪŋ]	für/mit wenig Geld
to **time** [taɪm]	den richtigen Zeitpunkt wählen
block [blɒk]	Block; Häuserblock
enthusiasm [ɪnˈθjuːziæzm]	Enthusiasmus; Begeisterung
just in time [ˌdʒʌst ɪn ˈtaɪm]	gerade rechtzeitig
sunset [ˈsʌnset]	Sonnenuntergang
to **sneak** [sniːk], **snuck** [snʌk], **snuck** [snʌk]	schleichen; schmuggeln
service [ˈsɜːvɪs]	Service; Dienstleistung; Dienst
Leave that to me. [ˌliːv ðæt tə ˈmiː]	Überlass das mir.
bright [braɪt]	hell; leuchtend; strahlend
tour company [ˈtʊə ˌkʌmpəni]	Reiseanbieter
to **be located** [bi ləʊˈkeɪtɪd]	gelegen sein; liegen
subway *(AE)* [ˈsʌbweɪ]	U-Bahn
to **groan** [grəʊn]	stöhnen

statue [ˈstætʃuː]	Statue; Standbild
liberty [ˈlɪbəti]	Freiheit
artist [ˈɑːtɪst]	Künstler/-in
tablet [ˈtæblət]	Tafel
spike [spaɪk]	Spitze; Stachel
to **base on** [ˈbeɪs ɒn]	stützen auf
goddess [ˈgɒdes]	Göttin
to **be known as** [bi ˈnəʊn əz]	bekannt sein als
enlightenment [ɪnˈlaɪtnmənt]	Aufklärung; Erleuchtung
ethnic [ˈeθnɪk]	ethnisch; Volks-; *hier:* exotisch
from the outside [ˌfrəm ðɪ aʊtˈsaɪd]	von außen
delicious [dɪˈlɪʃəs]	köstlich
fried [fraɪd]	gebraten *(in der Pfanne)*
pastry [ˈpeɪstri]	Teig; Teigtasche
filling [ˈfɪlɪŋ]	Füllung
Jewish [ˈdʒuːɪʃ]	jüdisch
truck *(AE)* [trʌk]	*hier:* Wagen
cart [kɑːt]	Karren
New Yorker [ˌnjuː ˈjɔːkə]	New Yorker/-in
to **combine** [kəmˈbaɪn]	kombinieren; verbinden
flavor *(AE)* [ˈfleɪvə]	Geschmack; Aroma
specialty *(AE)* [ˈspeʃlti]	Spezialität; Besonderheit
combination [ˌkɒmbɪˈneɪʃn]	Kombination; Verbindung
hometown [ˈhəʊmtaʊn]	Heimatstadt
spot [spɒt]	Fleck; Ort

3 Find the missing word

Put in the missing words.

1. London – Underground   New York – _____
2. house – architect   sculpture – _____
3. United States – states   New York – _____
4. money – bank   food / drinks – _____

4 In New York

Complete the words. They're all new in Station 1.

If you're out and about in New York on

a s _ _ _ _ _ _ _ _ _

and you're hungry, you can either go

to a d _ _ _ _ or buy a hot dog or

bagel from a food t _ _ _ _ or c _ _ _ .

Or what about a samosa – a

f _ _ _ _ p _ _ _ _ _ with a

vegetarian filling? In New York, you

can find e _ _ _ _ _ food from all

over the world. And New Yorkers are really creative in inventing new

food c _ _ _ _ _ _ _ _ _ _ _ . What do you think about a

cronut?!

5 What can you say?

You're visiting your aunt in New York. Write down what you say in English.

1. Du sagst, dass es super ist, dass sie sich den Tag freigenommen hat.

2. Du fragst, wo das Empire State Building liegt.

3. Du erzählst, dass du gelesen hast, dass Bedloe Island jetzt als „Liberty Island" bekannt ist.

4. In einem Diner sagst du, dass das Essen wirklich köstlich ist und dass ihr euch das Beste bis zum Schluss aufgehoben habt.

Station 2: Life is a trip

to **lift** [lɪft]	heben; hochheben; anheben
trunk *(AE)* [trʌŋk]	Kofferraum
to **be done with** [bi 'dʌn wɪð]	fertig sein mit
break [breɪk]	Durchbruch
rejection [rɪ'dʒektʃn]	Ablehnung; Absage
to **come true** [ˌkʌm 'truː]	wahr werden; in Erfüllung gehen
good luck [ˌgʊd 'lʌk]	(viel) Glück
sidewalk *(AE)* ['saɪdwɔːk]	Gehweg; Gehsteig
businessman ['bɪznɪsmæn]	Geschäftsmann
not necessarily [ˌnɒt nesə'serəli]	nicht notwendigerweise; nicht unbedingt
however [haʊ'evə]	jedoch
bill *(AE)* [bɪl]	Geldschein; Rechnung
change [tʃeɪndʒ]	Münzgeld; Wechselgeld
to **get in** [ˌget ˈɪn]	einsteigen
yet [jet]	doch; und trotzdem; und dennoch
to **complain** [kəm'pleɪn]	sich beschweren; sich beklagen
to **shop** [ʃɒp]	einkaufen; shoppen
needless to say [ˌniːdləs tə 'seɪ]	natürlich; selbstverständlich
tip [tɪp]	Trinkgeld
grade *(AE)* [greɪd]	Note
busker ['bʌskə]	Straßenmusikant/-in
to **perform** [pə'fɔːm]	aufführen; auftreten
freeway *(AE)* ['friːweɪ]	Autobahn
to **transport** [træn'spɔːt]	transportieren; befördern
lorry ['lɒri]	Lastwagen
to **fail to do sth** ['feɪl tə]	versäumen, etw. zu tun; es nicht schaffen, etw. zu tun
rags to riches [ˌrægz tə ˈrɪtʃɪz]	vom Tellerwäscher zum Millionär

to **make a living (from)** [ˌmeɪk ə ˈlɪvɪŋ frəm]	seinen Lebensunterhalt bestreiten (mit)
either ... or ... [ˈaɪðə/ˈiːðə ... ɔː]	entweder ... oder ...

6 Money, money, money

Put in the correct 'money' words.

1. The first guest at the Diner paid with a large

   _____, so Diego had almost no

   _____ left.

2. He was given a big _____ from the

   businessman who had just come in for a coffee.

3. He was very happy about that because his parents couldn't

   give him very much _____.

   Most of his friends were getting much more every month.

4. Sometimes guests from abroad wanted to pay in foreign

   _____.

   But Diego's boss didn't want

   him to accept these.

7 Bye bye, Lea!

Put in the correct verbs in the correct tense.

| complain | come true | inspire | shop | lift |
| perform | gasp | get in |

Rylee's dad _____ Lea's suitcase into the trunk of his car. They all _____ and drove to the airport. "It's sad I have to leave," Lea said. "But my dream _____: I've been to New York!" "Look at that busker," Rylee said. "It must be hard to _____ on the street every day." Rylee's mum smiled: "So you two have no reason to _____, do you? You do well at school, and you've got pocket money so that you can go downtown to _____ …" Suddenly they saw the Statue of Liberty right in front of them in the sunset. Lea _____. "That's a great view to say goodbye to New York," she said. "Maybe it _____ you to write a poem," Rylee's dad joked. "Why not?" Lea answered, and she was serious.

Story: Asphalt Tribe

panel ['pænl]	Bild *(eines Comics)*
lead-in ['liːdɪn]	Einführung; Einleitung
shape [ʃeɪp]	Form
sequence ['siːkwəns]	Abfolge; Reihenfolge
consecutive [kənˈsekjʊtɪv]	aufeinanderfolgend; fortlaufend
to **overlap** [ˌəʊvəˈlæp]	(sich) überlappen
to **lay** [leɪ], **laid** [leɪd], **laid** [leɪd]	legen
to **make use of** [meɪk ˈjuːz əv]	benutzen; verwenden
long shot [ˈlɒŋ ʃɒt]	Totale *(Kameraeinstellung)*
medium shot [ˈmiːdiəm ʃɒt]	Halbtotale *(Kameraeinstellung)*
medium [ˈmiːdiəm]	mittel; mittelgroß
effect [ɪˈfekt]	Effekt; Wirkung
stylistic [staɪˈlɪstɪk]	Stil-; stilistisch
speed [spiːd]	Geschwindigkeit

8 Say it in a different way

Write down the missing word or phrase to make a sentence with a similar meaning.

1. This car is driving very fast.

   → This car is driving at high _____.

2. I like the introduction to the story.

   → I like the _____ to the story.

3. They put their raincoats on the bed.

   → They _____ their raincoats

   on the bed.

9 Graphic novels

Put in the correct words.

A graphic novel is divided into individual _____ which can be of different sizes and _____. But the story is not only told by pictures, but also by speech or thought bubbles and _____. Sometimes the panels are not arranged consecutively, but they _____. This special _____ makes graphic novels interesting to read, just like the different kinds of shots. There can be _____ or _____ shots and close-ups. All of them have different _____ – some create suspense, for example; others make the reader experience the story.

10 Synonyms

Write down a word with the same or a similar meaning.

1. picture ⟶ _____
2. to stage ⟶ _____
3. to buy ⟶ _____

Action USA! New Yorkers don't do things like that!

to **cringe** [krɪndʒ]	schaudern; sich ducken
unexpected [ˌʌnɪkˈspektɪd]	unerwartet

Skills: How to conduct a podcast interview

to **conduct** [kənˈdʌkt]	durchführen; ausführen
path [pɑːθ]	Pfad; Weg
follow-up [ˈfɒləʊʌp]	Fortsetzung; Folge-
talk [tɔːk]	Gespräch; Unterhaltung

11 Word families: Questions and answers

Complete the sentences with a word from the same word family.

1. Did you **expect** your grandparents today? – No, it was an

   _____ visit!

2. In your _____, remember to ask

   Daniel Radcliffe about the Quidditch scenes. – Good idea!

   A question like that should immediately **follow** the small talk

   at the beginning.

3. The students I interviewed **talked** a lot about their problems

   with cyber bullying. – So it was really important that you held

   this _____ !

4. You used interesting **stylistic** elements in your text. – OK!

   Do you think I need to improve the _____

   of the text in any way?

12 Phrases for interviews

Write down two phrases each for the different stages of an interview.

1. Small talk: _____

2. Follow-up: _____

3. Getting specific: _____

4. Open questions: _____

5. At the end: _____

13 Check on your ... AE spelling

Write down the AE words you've learned so far that are spelled differently from the BE spelling.

Text smart 2 Internet texts

Tip

Wenn du dir bei der Aussprache bestimmter Wörter nicht sicher bist, schlage sie in einem Online-Wörterbuch nach. Denn dort kannst du dir auch die Aussprache anhören – in BE und AE.

Introduction

reliable [rɪˈlaɪəbl]	verlässlich; zuverlässig; vertrauenswürdig
inconvenient [ˌɪnkənˈviːniənt]	unbequem; lästig
up-to-date [ˌʌptəˈdeɪt]	modern; zeitgemäß; aktuell
tutorial [tjuːˈtɔːriəl]	Tutorium; Tutorial
moon landing [ˈmuːn ˌlændɪŋ]	Mondlandung
science [saɪəns]	Wissenschaft; Naturwissenschaft
astronaut [ˈæstrənɔːt]	Astronaut/-in
human [ˈhjuːmən]	Mensch
to **be considered (to be)** sth [bi kənˈsɪdəd tə]	als etw. gelten

TS 2

1 Internet vocabulary

Draw lines to match the verbs and nouns or phrases that are often used together.

1. watch
2. post
3. stay
4. get
5. do
6. follow

a) up-to-date on social media

b) quick information with apps

c) blogs

d) research for school projects on science websites

e) a comment

f) tutorials

2 Odd word out

Cross out the word that doesn't fit.

1. human | person | machine | man
2. up-to-date | reliable | inconvenient | sequence
3. astronaut | panel | moon landing | rock
4. effect | tutorial | blog | social media website
5. science | discovery | talk | invention
6. speed | fast | quick | shape
7. medium | small | media | large
8. freeway | path | road | street

Station 1: An online wiki text

wiki (text)	[ˈwɪki ˌtekst]	Wikitext
mission	[ˈmɪʃn]	Mission; Auftrag
to touch down	[tʌtʃ ˈdaʊn]	landen
surface	[ˈsɜːfɪs]	Oberfläche
to announce	[əˈnaʊns]	ankündigen; durchsagen
to step	[step]	treten; steigen
president	[ˈprezɪdnt]	Präsident/-in
priority	[praɪˈɒrəti]	Priorität; Vorrang
to challenge	[ˈtʃælɪndʒ]	herausfordern
engineer	[ˌendʒɪˈnɪə]	Ingenieur/-in; Techniker/-in
political	[pəˈlɪtɪkl]	politisch
hoax	[həʊks]	Täuschung; Trick
conspiracy	[kənˈspɪrəsi]	Verschwörung
theory	[ˈθɪəri]	Theorie
to stage	[steɪdʒ]	inszenieren; aufführen
the public	[ðə ˈpʌblɪk]	die Öffentlichkeit
to involve	[ɪnˈvɒlv]	involvieren; einbeziehen; beteiligen
cover-up	[ˈkʌvərʌp]	Vertuschung
government	[ˈgʌvnmənt]	Regierung
complicated	[ˈkɒmplɪkeɪtɪd]	kompliziert
impossible	[ɪmˈpɒsəbl]	unmöglich
to make sense	[ˌmeɪk ˈsens]	Sinn ergeben; einleuchten
at the time	[ˌət ðə ˈtaɪm]	damals
to run	[rʌn]	betreiben; leiten; führen
tech	[tek]	Technologie; Technik
respect	[rɪˈspekt]	Respekt
entertaining	[ˌentəˈteɪnɪŋ]	unterhaltsam
function	[ˈfʌŋkʃn]	Funktion
to trick	[trɪk]	austricksen; täuschen

to **estimate** [ˈestɪmeɪt]	schätzen
to **question** [ˈkwestʃən]	fragen; hinterfragen
critical [ˈkrɪtɪkl]	kritisch

3 What do they do?

Complete the descriptions with the correct jobs.

1. An _____ invents new machines or computer programmes.

2. A _____ is the head of state or the head of a company.

3. A _____ does research to make new discoveries in medicine or biology, for example.

4. An _____ creates print, online or TV ads for new products.

5. A _____ interviews people and writes articles.

TS 2

4 Wiki text vs. blog post

Write the words or phrases in the correct part of the grid.

- entertaining
- factual
- plays a trick on somebody
- questions somebody's motivations
- informative
- stages a hoax
- reliable
- believable

Wiki text	Blog post

5 Opposites

Find the opposite of each word.

1. possible _____

2. boring _____

3. beautiful _____

4. animal _____

Station 2: Online ratings

to **rate** [reɪt]	bewerten; einstufen
space [speɪs]	Weltraum; Weltall
space program ['speɪs ˌprəʊɡræm]	Raumfahrtprogramm
breathtaking ['breθˌteɪkɪŋ]	atemberaubend
well-written [ˌwel'rɪtn]	gut geschrieben
disappointing [ˌdɪsə'pɔɪntɪŋ]	enttäuschend
special effect [ˌspeʃl ɪ'fekt]	Spezialeffekt
well-developed [ˌweldɪ'veləpt]	gut entwickelt; ausgereift
undeveloped [ˌʌndɪ'veləpt]	unentwickelt; unausgereift
badly-written [ˌbædli'rɪtn]	schlecht geschrieben
weak [wiːk]	schwach

6 Make new words

Use the prefixes or suffixes to form adjectives.

Prefixes/suffixes: dis-, un-, in-, im-, -y, -less

Words: developed, honest, possible, luck, secure, realistic, expected, health, use, end

1. _____
2. _____
3. _____
4. _____
5. _____
6. _____
7. _____
8. _____
9. _____
10. _____

7 An online rating

Put in the correct words.

`breathtaking` `weak` `special effects` `well-developed` `believable` `space`

Lost on the Moon is the best movie set in

_____ I've ever seen. It's full of

action, suspense and _____.

_____ characters make

the story _____, and

_____ visuals hooked me

from the first minute. Only the costumes are rather

_____ – they should definitely be

more up-to date.

8 Check on your … science vocabulary

Make a list of the science words you've learned in Text smart 2. Then add those from Green Line 3.

_____

_____

_____

_____

AC3

Across cultures 3 What you say and how you say it

> **Tip**
>
> Sprich dir deine Vokabeln ab und zu laut vor, oder lass sie dir von Freunden, Geschwistern oder deinen Eltern vorlesen. So kannst du sie dir noch besser merken.

register [ˈredʒɪstə]	Sprachebene; Register
Canadian [kəˈneɪdiən]	kanadisch; Kanadier/-in
to **pronounce** [prəˈnaʊns]	aussprechen
schedule *(AE)* [ˈʃedjuːl; ˈskedʒuːl]	Stundenplan; Fahrplan; Terminkalender
though [ðəʊ]	doch; jedoch; obwohl
water fountain [ˈwɔːtə ˌfaʊntɪn]	Wasserspender
informal [ɪnˈfɔːml]	informell; zwanglos
nope *(infml)* [nəʊp]	nee; nö
It sucks. *(slang)* [ɪt ˈsʌks]	Das ist zum Kotzen.
ain't (= isn't/aren't) [eɪnt]	ist nicht; sind nicht
totally [ˈtəʊtli]	völlig; total
whatever [wɒtˈevə]	was/wie auch immer; egal (was/welche)
no more [ˌnəʊ ˈmɔː]	nicht mehr
(I) didn't mean to … [aɪ ˌdɪdnt ˈmiːn tə]	Ich wollte nicht …
auntie [ˈɑːnti]	Tantchen
not … either [nɒt … ˈaɪðə; nɒt … ˈiːðə]	auch nicht
to **mind** sth [maɪnd]	auf etw. aufpassen

AC 3

1 Which register?

Put in the correct phrase in the correct register.

It's so wild to see you again | it sucks | I don't go there anymore

It was, like, so totally not my thing | I'm sorry

1. Old lady: Be careful, young man! You just stepped on my foot!

   Boy: Oh, _____.

2. Girl: I don't want to do that Maths homework. It's too much!

   Boy: Yeah, _____!

3. Callum: Did you like the film we watched last night?

   Tristan: Nope. _____.

4. Tristan's grandad: I think you need to leave now for your soccer training.

   Tristan: _____.

   I've started to play baseball and I like it better!

5. Sophie: Hi Matt! What's up?

   Matt: Hi! _____!

51

AC 3

2 Pronunciation: AE or BE?

Read the words in the phonetic alphabet and write them down. Add if they're AE or BE too.

1. [nuːz] _____ __
2. [dɒg] _____ __
3. [noʊ] _____ __
4. [bɑːθ] _____ __
5. [wɜːrk] _____ __
6. [æsk] _____ __

3 Where are they from?

Make adjectives from the country names and use them to complete the sentences.

Britain   Germany   the US   France   Canada

1. Many ice hockey players in Germany are _____.

2. The players of the _____ national football team usually wear white shirts.

3. _____ cheese is famous all over the world.

4. Most _____ students take the Pledge of Allegiance every morning.

5. _____ students are used to wearing school uniforms.

Unit 3 A nation invents itself

> **Tip**
>
> Du kannst dein Hörverstehen auch beim Surfen im Internet trainieren, z. B. wenn du ein Tutorial auf Englisch anschaust. Achte darauf, dass der Sprecher / die Sprecherin ein Muttersprachler ist. Du hörst dann echtes gesprochenes Englisch. Wenn du nicht alle Wörter kennst, kannst du dir ihre Bedeutung erschließen, denn du siehst, was im Video getan wird.

nation [ˈneɪʃn]	Nation

Introduction

innovation [ˌɪnəˈveɪʃn]	Innovation; Neuerung
transportation *(AE)* [ˌtrænspɔːˈteɪʃn]	Transport
innovative [ɪˈnəʊvətɪv; ˈɪnəvətɪv]	innovativ; kreativ
after [ˈɑːftə]	nachdem
to **colonize** *(AE)* [ˈkɒlənaɪz]	kolonisieren
permanent [ˈpɜːmnənt]	permanent; dauerhaft
settlement [ˈsetlmənt]	Siedlung
by the time [ˌbaɪ ðə ˈtaɪm]	bis *(zu dem Zeitpunkt)*
eastern [ˈiːstn]	östlich; Ost-
to **declare** [dɪˈkleə]	erklären
to **treat** [triːt]	behandeln
army [ˈɑːmi]	Armee
general [ˈdʒenrl]	General
settler [ˈsetlə]	Siedler/-in
to **suffer (from)** [ˈsʌfə frəm]	leiden (unter)

peak [piːk]	Haupt-; Spitzen-
a total of [ə ˈtəʊtl̩ əv]	insgesamt
to **pass** [pɑːs]	durchgehen; vorbeigehen (an); passieren
united [juːˈnaɪtɪd]	vereint; vereinigt
stranger [ˈstreɪndʒə]	Fremde/-r
especially [ɪˈspeʃli]	besonders; vor allem
to **descend from** [dɪˈsend frəm]	abstammen von; herstammen von
belongings *(pl)* [bɪˈlɒŋɪŋz]	Habseligkeiten; Hab und Gut
covered wagon [ˌkʌvəd ˈwæɡən]	Planwagen

1 Odd word out

Cross out the word that doesn't fit.

1. transportation | covered wagon | army | subway
2. colonize | settlement | found | pass
3. stranger | foreign | declare | immigrant
4. divided | group | united | together

2 American history words

Make a list of the words you've learned in the Introduction to talk about American history.

_____

_____

_____

_____

3 European settlement in America

Complete the text with words from the same word families as the words in brackets.

America was _____ (colony) by immigrants

from Europe. The first _____ (settlement)

in North America were English. The immigrants could not

bring many of their _____ (to belong to)

because the ships were crowded. The long journey was hard,

_____ (special) for small children – they had

no idea about their new life in America.

At the beginning of the 19th century, more and more settlers

moved to the West. _____ (to transport)

was much more difficult at that time than it is today: People were

crushed in tiny covered wagons. The Native Americans suffered

badly from the European settlement – many were killed, and many

others lost their _____ (tradition) lands.

Today the US is known as a country of _____

(innovative) . The reason for this can be found in the country's

_____ (historical).

Station 1: This story sounds great!

bat [bæt]	Schläger *(Tischtennis; Baseball)*
last name *(AE)* ['lɑːst neɪm]	Nachname; Familienname
to pass [pɑːs]	bestehen
medical ['medɪkl]	medizinisch; ärztlich; Medizin-
examination [ɪɡˌzæmɪ'neɪʃn]	Untersuchung; Prüfung
to disappear [ˌdɪsə'pɪə]	verschwinden
great-great-grandfather [ˌɡreɪtɡreɪt'ɡrænˌfɑːðə]	Ururgroßvater
terrible ['terəbl]	schrecklich; schlimm; furchtbar
to catch an infection [ɪn'fekʃn]	sich eine Infektion holen; sich einen Infekt holen
calm [kɑːm]	ruhig; friedlich
drinking water ['drɪŋkɪŋ ˌwɔːtə]	Trinkwasser
in fact [ɪn 'fækt]	tatsächlich; eigentlich; genau genommen
to manage (to do sth) ['mænɪdʒ tə]	schaffen (etw. zu tun)
reservation [ˌrezə'veɪʃn]	Reservat
to recognize *(AE)* ['rekəɡnaɪz]	erkennen; anerkennen
in addition to [ɪn əˈdɪʃn tə]	neben; daneben; darüber hinaus
to comfort ['kʌmfət]	trösten; ermutigen
frightened ['fraɪtnd]	verängstigt
relieved [rɪ'liːvd]	erleichtert
exhausting [ɪɡ'zɔːstɪŋ]	anstrengend
had gotten off *(AE)* [hæd ˌɡɒtnˈɒf]	waren ausgestiegen
papers *(pl)* ['peɪpəz]	Unterlagen; Papiere
to start all over again [ˌstɑːt ɔːl ˈəʊvər əˌɡen]	ganz von vorn beginnen
statistics *(pl)* [stə'tɪstɪks]	Statistik

table ['teɪbl]	Tabelle
bar graph ['bɑː grɑːf]	Säulendiagramm; Balkendiagramm
line graph ['laɪn grɑːf]	Kurvendiagramm
pie chart ['paɪ ˌtʃɑːt]	Kuchendiagramm; Tortendiagramm
to **publish** ['pʌblɪʃ]	veröffentlichen; publizieren; verlegen
majority [məˈdʒɒrəti]	Mehrheit; Mehrzahl
minority [maɪˈnɒrəti]	Minderheit
percent, percent *(pl)* [pəˈsent]	Prozent
to **grow by** ['grəʊ baɪ]	steigen um
to **suggest** [səˈdʒest]	andeuten; nahelegen
conclusion [kənˈkluːʒn]	Schluss; Schlussfolgerung

4 Health words

Put in the correct words. Their first letters help you.

1. Ursula: After the m_____ e_____

    at Ellis Island, I was sent back because I'd

    c_____ an eye i_____ .

2. Johan: Some children got s_____ on the way to

    America because the drinking water was dirty.

3. Tim: I think I've caught a cold. I have a c_____

    and my hands are really cold. Maybe I have a

    f_____ too.

3

5 Word search: Statistics words

Find seven statistics words (→, ↓ or ↘) and write four of them below the correct pictures.

T	W	T	H	J	L	O	M	P	Y
C	A	B	A	R	G	R	A	P	H
X	B	B	M	P	U	I	J	L	F
F	M	J	L	V	X	E	O	Z	I
P	E	R	C	E	N	T	R	Y	G
I	P	R	W	Q	A	E	I	J	U
P	I	E	C	H	A	R	T	I	R
M	I	N	O	R	I	T	Y	P	E

1. _____

2. _____

3. _____

4. _____

Station 2: Necessity is the mother of invention

necessity [nə'sesəti]	Notwendigkeit
communications network [kə‚mju:nɪ'keɪʃnz ‚netwɜ:k]	Kommunikationsnetz; Nachrichtennetz
face-to-face [‚feɪs tə 'feɪs]	von Angesicht zu Angesicht; Auge in Auge
to **migrate** [maɪ'greɪt]	wandern; umherziehen
pioneer [‚paɪə'nɪə]	Pionier/-in
western ['westən]	westlich; West-
mass migration [‚mæs maɪ'greɪʃn]	Massenwanderung
to **expand** [ɪk'spænd]	(sich) ausdehnen; erweitern
wanted ['wɒntɪd]	gesucht
skinny ['skɪni]	dünn; mager
fellow ['feləʊ]	Bursche; Kerl
rider ['raɪdə]	Reiter/-in; Fahrer/-in
to **risk** [rɪsk]	riskieren
mail [meɪl]	Post
to **employ** [ɪm'plɔɪ]	einstellen; anstellen; beschäftigen
as [æz; əz]	da; weil
even though [‚i:vn 'ðəʊ]	auch wenn; obwohl
to **replace (by/with)** [rɪ'pleɪs]	ersetzen (durch)
to **develop** [dɪ'veləp]	(sich) entwickeln
to **connect (to)** [kə'nekt tə]	verbinden (mit); vermitteln; anschließen
instantly ['ɪnstəntli]	sofort
long-lasting ['lɒŋlɑ:stɪŋ]	lang anhaltend
in order to [ɪn ‚ɔ:də tə]	um ... zu; mit der Absicht
to **start off** [‚stɑ:t 'ɒf]	anfangen; beginnen; starten
motor car ['məʊtə ‚kɑ:]	Automobil
motion picture [‚məʊʃn 'pɪktʃə]	Film; Spielfilm
importance [ɪm'pɔ:tns]	Bedeutung; Wichtigkeit

colonial [kəˈləʊniəl]	kolonial; Kolonial-
spirit [ˈspɪrɪt]	Geist; Stimmung
to **shape** [ʃeɪp]	formen
barbecue [ˈbɑːbɪkjuː]	Grill(party)
stripe [straɪp]	Streifen

Skills: How to write a report

grandmother [ˈɡrænˌmʌðə]	Großmutter
insurance [ɪnˈʃʊərns]	Versicherung

Unit task: Oral historian for a day

oral [ˈɔːrl]	mündlich
historian [hɪˈstɔːriən]	Historiker/-in

6 Migration words

Write the words in the correct part of the grid. One word fits in two categories.

- expand
- wanted
- migrate
- pioneer
- rider
- colonial
- colonize
- mass migration
- risk
- western
- eastern

Nouns	Verbs	Adjectives

7 Opposites

Find the opposite of each word.

1. grandfather ⤳ _____
2. minority ⤳ _____
3. introduction ⤳ _____
4. nervous ⤳ _____
5. formal ⤳ _____

8 Word families: Nouns and adjectives

Complete the grid with the correct nouns or adjectives.

Nouns	Adjectives
	important
colony	
medicine	
	national
	historical
entertainment	

9 Word friends

Draw lines to match the nouns that belong together.

1. oral
2. insurance
3. communications
4. motion
5. motor
6. mass

a) network
b) historian
c) migration
d) office
e) picture
f) car

Story: A journey into the unknown

the unknown [ðɪ ˌʌnˈnəʊn]	das Unbekannte
Ma [mɑː]	Mama
to **come up to** [ˌkʌm ˈʌp tə]	zukommen auf
to **keep a diary** [ˌkiːp ə ˈdaɪəri]	ein Tagebuch führen
apart [əˈpɑːt]	auseinander; getrennt
Pa [pɑː]	Papa
trail [treɪl]	Weg; Pfad
preparation [ˌprepəˈreɪʃn]	Vorbereitung
to **head (for)** [ˈhed fə]	zusteuern auf
to **farm** [fɑːm]	Landwirtschaft betreiben
by *(+ gerund)* [baɪ]	indem
to **wave** [weɪv]	winken; schwenken
to **pack** [pæk]	packen; einpacken
grass [grɑːs]	Gras
furniture *(singular noun with plural meaning)* [ˈfɜːnɪtʃə]	Möbel
to **abandon** [əˈbændən]	aufgeben; zurücklassen
proper [ˈprɒpə]	richtig; ordentlich; angemessen
to **own** [əʊn]	besitzen
to **wonder** [ˈwʌndə]	sich Gedanken machen; sich fragen
up to [ˈʌp tə]	bis zu
chest [tʃest]	Brust; Brustkorb
to **join in** [ˌdʒɔɪn ˈɪn]	teilnehmen; mitmachen
bottom [ˈbɒtəm]	Boden; unterer Teil; Grund
flour [flaʊə]	Mehl
to **reach (for)** [ˈriːtʃ fə]	greifen (nach)
spicy [ˈspaɪsi]	würzig; pikant
Russian [ˈrʌʃn]	Russe/Russin; russisch; Russisch
in spite of [ɪn ˈspaɪt əv]	trotz

recent ['ri:snt]	kürzlich; neueste/-r/-s; letzte/-r/-s
alive [ə'laɪv]	lebend; am Leben; lebendig
to **get well** [ˌget 'wel]	gesund werden
none [nʌn]	keine/-r/-s
herd [hɜ:d]	Herde; Rudel
bison ['baɪsn], **bison** ['baɪsn] *(pl)*	Bison; Büffel
to **be stuck** [bi 'stʌk]	festsitzen; feststecken; hängen bleiben

Action USA! America: A big salad bowl?

honor *(AE)* ['ɒnə]	Ehre
equal ['i:kwəl]	gleich; gleichwertig
no matter [nəʊ 'mætə]	egal; ganz gleich

10 A journey into the unknown: Verbs

Put in the correct verbs in the correct tense.

One day Lilly's mother _____ her, holding a book

in her hands. She wants her to _____ a diary.

A few weeks later, the family _____ West.

Lilly's father thinks that there is space and lots of land to

_____ . So they all _____ their things

and argue about what to take and what to leave. They pass some

furniture someone _____ in the grass, and they

_____ why people who _____

a piano were out on the Oregon Trail.

11 Jumbled sentences

Find the right word order and make sentences.

1. here | I | trail | why | folks | were | rich | out | on | wonder | the

   _____

   _____

2. too | mud | hard | drive | to | wagons | raining | through | the | the | it's

   _____

   _____

3. writing | you | I | continue | Abbie's | think | should | diary

   _____

   _____

12 Check on your ... history vocabulary

Make a list of the British history words from Green Line 3.

_____

_____

_____

_____

Text smart 3 Travel texts

> **Tip**
>
> Hast du ein Traum-Reiseziel? Dann such doch mal nach englischsprachigen Texten darüber im Internet, oder nach einem Reiseführer auf Englisch in der Bücherei. So verbindest du Informationen, die dich interessieren, mit der Erweiterung deines Wortschatzes.

Introduction

incredible [ɪnˈkredəbl]	unglaublich
to **scare sb to death** [ˌskeə tə ˈdeθ]	jmdn. zu Tode erschrecken
to **fear** [fɪə]	(sich) fürchten
heat *(no pl)* [hiːt]	Hitze; Wärme
to **be aware of sth** [bi ə'weər əv]	sich etw. bewusst sein
rough [rʌf]	rau; grob; uneben; holprig
reception [rɪˈsepʃn]	Empfang
to **educate** [ˈedʒʊkeɪt]	erziehen; bilden
to **meet sb's expectations** [ˌmiːt sʌmbədiz ˌekspekˈteɪʃnz]	jmds. Erwartungen erfüllen

TS 3

1 Phrases

Complete the sentences with the correct phrases. Make sure you use the correct tenses and personal pronouns.

`be aware of sth`   `scare sb to death`   `start all over again`
`catch an infection`   `meet sb's expectations`

1. Suddenly I saw a bison. It was running towards me.

   It _____ !

2. I'd read a lot about New York before I went there, and the

   city really _____ .

3. Visitors to Death Valley must _____

   _____ several dangers: the heat,

   the spiders and the roads.

4. European settlers had to _____

   _____ in America.

5. Many immigrants _____

   on the crowded ships from Europe to America.

Station 1: A travel guide

general ['dʒenrl]	allgemein
snow-capped ['snəʊkæpt]	schneebedeckt
summit ['sʌmɪt]	Gipfel; Berggipfel
turbulent ['tɜːbjələnt]	turbulent; aufgewühlt
glacial ['gleɪsɪəl; 'gleɪʃl]	eisig; Gletscher-
valley ['væli]	Tal
wooded ['wʊdɪd]	bewaldet
sparkling ['spɑːklɪŋ]	glitzernd; funkelnd
to **hunt** [hʌnt]	jagen
snow tire *(AE)* ['snəʊ ˌtaɪə]	Winterreifen
grizzly bear ['grɪzli ˌbeə]	Grizzlybär
elk [elk]	Elch
bighorn sheep [ˌbɪghɔːn 'ʃiːp]	Dickhornschaf
chain [tʃeɪn]	Kette
dusty ['dʌsti]	staubig
enjoyable [ɪn'dʒɔɪəbl]	angenehm; unterhaltsam
copper-mining ['kɒpəˌmaɪnɪŋ]	Kupferbergbau

2 Word friends: Montana

Draw lines to match the adjectives and nouns that belong together.

1. snow-capped   a) lakes
2. glacial   b) summits
3. turbulent   c) valleys
4. dusty   d) rivers
5. sparkling   e) prairie

Station 2: A travel blog

to **hitchhike** [ˈhɪtʃhaɪk]	trampen; per Anhalter fahren
hitchhiking [ˈhɪtʃhaɪkɪŋ]	Trampen
to **get a ride** [ˌget ə ˈraɪd]	eine Mitfahrgelegenheit bekommen
truck *(AE)* [trʌk]	Truck; Lastwagen
hitchhiker [ˈhɪtʃhaɪkə]	Tramper/-in
edge of town [ˌedʒ əv ˈtaʊn]	Stadtrand
parking lot [ˈpɑːkɪŋ ˌlɒt]	Parkplatz
cardboard [ˈkɑːdbɔːd]	Pappe; Karton
to **stick out** [ˌstɪk ˈaʊt], stuck out [ˌstʌk ˈaʊt], stuck out [ˌstʌk ˈaʊt]	hinausstrecken
backseat [ˈbæksiːt]	Rücksitz
to **murder** [ˈmɜːdə]	ermorden; umbringen
to **rob** [rɒb]	ausrauben; rauben; berauben
kitty litter [ˈkɪti ˌlɪtə]	Katzenstreu
passenger seat [ˈpæsndʒə ˌsiːt]	Beifahrersitz
unless [ənˈles]	es sei denn, (dass) …; wenn nicht
creature [ˈkriːtʃə]	Kreatur; Lebewesen; Geschöpf
seat belt [ˈsiːt belt]	Sicherheitsgurt
to **run over** [ˌrʌn ˈəʊvə]	überfahren
to **drop sb off** [ˌdrɒp ˈɒf]	jmdn. absetzen; jmdn. aussteigen lassen
storyteller [ˈstɔːriˌtelə]	Geschichtenerzähler/-in

3 A mind map: On the road

Make a mind map with verbs, nouns and adjectives you can use to talk about being on the road.

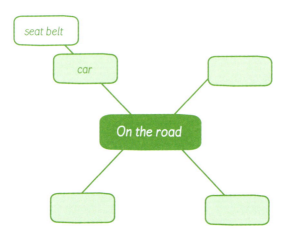

4 Check on your ... travel words

Make lists for the two word groups.

Transportation: _____

_____

_____

Nature: _____

_____

_____

Across cultures 4
At home with an American family

> **Tip**
>
> Schau dir mal die Lebensmittel-Verpackungen an, die ihr zu Hause habt. Oft stehen dort die Zutaten und Inhaltsstoffe auch auf Englisch. Lies sie dir durch. Welche Wörter kennst du, welche sind neu?

household [ˈhaʊshəʊld]	Haushalt
chore [tʃɔː]	(lästige) Pflicht; Bürde
to **set the table** [ˌset ðə ˈteɪbl]	den Tisch decken
to **vacuum** [ˈvækjuːm]	staubsaugen
to **load** [ləʊd]	einräumen; laden
to **empty** [ˈemti]	leeren; ausräumen
to **clean up** [ˌkliːn ˈʌp]	aufräumen; sauber machen
dishwasher [ˈdɪʃwɒʃə]	Spülmaschine
to **do the dishes** [ˌduː ðə ˈdɪʃɪz]	den Abwasch machen
dishes *(pl)* [ˈdɪʃɪz]	Geschirr
garbage *(AE)* [ˈɡɑːbɪdʒ]	Müll; Abfall
rug [rʌɡ]	Vorleger; Teppich
allowance *(AE)* [əˈlaʊəns]	Taschengeld
to **obey** [əˈbeɪ]	gehorchen
preference [ˈprefrns]	Vorliebe
issue [ˈɪʃuː; ˈɪsjuː]	Abneigung; Problem

AC 4

1 Find the verbs: Household chores

Put in the correct verbs to complete the collocations.

1. Callum: Can I help you? I could _____ the dishwasher.

2. Tristan's mom: The dishes are already clean. But you can _____ the dishwasher. Tristan, can you _____ your room, please? The floor is really dusty.

3. Tristan: OK. Do you want me to _____ the garbage _____ too?

4. Tristan's mom: No thanks, I'll do that. But can you two _____ the table, please?

2 Jumbled words: At home

Put the letters in the correct order to make words.

1. LOSEUHOHD

   _____

2. HIDESS

   _____

3. MUVCAU

   _____

4. CEHRO

   _____

Unit 4 The Pacific Northwest

> **Tip**
>
> Lerne Redewendungen am besten in ganzen Sätzen, damit du gleich weißt, wie du sie anwenden musst.

Introduction

to **consist of** [kənˈsɪstˌəv]	bestehen aus
boomtown [ˈbuːmtaʊn]	schnell wachsende Stadt
orca [ˈɔːkə]	Schwertwal
cougar [ˈkuːɡə]	Puma; Berglöwe
wolf [wʊlf], **wolves** [wʊlvz] *(pl)*	Wolf
native [ˈneɪtɪv]	einheimisch; eingeboren
volcano [vɒlˈkeɪnəʊ], **volcanoes** [vɒlˈkeɪnəʊz] *(pl)*	Vulkan
economy [ɪˈkɒnəmi]	Ökonomie; Wirtschaft
growth [ɡrəʊθ]	Wachstum
corporation [ˌkɔːprˈeɪʃn]	Konzern; Unternehmen
total [ˈtəʊtl]	gesamt; Gesamt-
employee [ɪmˈplɔɪiː]	Angestellte/-r; Mitarbeiter/-in; Arbeitnehmer/-in
airplane [ˈeəpleɪn]	Flugzeug
retail [ˈriːteɪl]	Einzelhandel
waterfront [ˈwɔːtəfrʌnt]	Hafenviertel; Ufer
the outdoors [ði ˌaʊtˈdɔːz]	die Natur

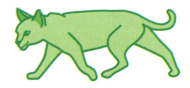

4

1 Definitions

Put in the correct words.

1. A _____ is a kind of big wild cat.

2. Somebody who works for a company or business and is employed is an _____.

3. Plants and flowers that are _____ to a region are typical for the area.

4. The part of a town that is close to the sea or a river is called the _____.

5. An _____ is a big, black and white animal that lives in the water and is native to the Pacific Northwest.

6. '_____' is another word for 'nature'.

7. A _____ is a city that grows very fast.

Station 1: You've got no soul!

You've got no soul! [juːv ˌgɒt nəʊ ˈsəʊl]	*hier:* Du hast kein Feingefühl!
soul [səʊl]	Seele
wilderness [ˈwɪldənəs]	Wildnis
national park [ˌnæʃnl ˈpɑːk]	Nationalpark; Naturpark
peace [piːs]	Frieden
calm [kɑːm]	Ruhe
great wheel [ˌgreɪt ˈwiːl]	Riesenrad
to **be true to oneself** [bi ˈtruː tu wʌnˌself]	sich selbst treu bleiben
part-time [ˌpɑːtˈtaɪm]	Teilzeit-; Halbtags-
kind of [ˈkaɪnd ˌəv]	ziemlich
to **be in a hurry** [ˌbi ɪn ə ˈhʌri]	es eilig haben; in Eile sein
waiter [ˈweɪtə]	Kellner/-in; Bedienung
It's my treat. [ɪts ˈmaɪ ˌtriːt]	Das geht auf meine Rechnung.
unbelievable [ˌʌnbɪˈliːvəbl]	unglaublich; unglaubwürdig
deal [diːl]	Abmachung; Übereinkunft
to **hold a competition** [ˌhəʊld ə ˌkɒmpəˈtɪʃn]	einen Wettbewerb durchführen
entry [ˈentri]	Beitrag; Einsendung
hydroplane [ˈhaɪdrəpleɪn]	Gleitboot
rubber raft [ˌrʌbə ˈrɑːft]	Schlauchboot
happiness [ˈhæpɪnəs]	Glück; Zufriedenheit; Fröhlichkeit
major [ˈmeɪdʒə]	wichtig; bedeutend; Haupt-
paddleboard [ˈpædlbɔːd]	Paddling Board *(eine Art Surfbrett, auf dem man aufrecht stehend paddelt)*
to **protect sb/sth (from)** [prəˈtekt frəm]	jmdn./etw. (be)schützen (vor)
to **buy time** [ˌbaɪ ˈtaɪm]	Zeit gewinnen

Just a second ... [ˌdʒʌst ə 'seknd]	Einen Augenblick ...
second ['seknd]	Sekunde
nature lover ['neɪtʃə ˌlʌvə]	Naturfreund/-in

2 Different situations

Write down sentences you could say in the following situations.

1. Your're on a hiking tour with your family, and your mom admires the great view of a mountain chain. Your brother says that he's hungry.

   You: _____ !

2. Your best friend pretends that he/she loves rap music because he/she wants to impress the cool new boy/girl at school.

   You: _____ !

3. You run for the bus because you're late. Your neighbor says "Hi!" and wants to start a conversation.

   You: I'm sorry, I can't talk now.

   _____ !

3 Say it in a different way

Write down the missing word or phrase to make a sentence with a similar meaning.

1. I only work half-days.

   → My job is a _____ job.

2. I'm going to pay the bill today.

   → _____ today.

3. Student motivation was an important topic at the teachers' conference.

   → Student motivation was a _____ topic at the teachers' conference.

4. To get a bit of time to think about my arguments, I asked the others to have a short break.

   → To _____, I asked the others to have a short break.

5. I don't have much time.

   → I'm _____.

6. It's quite a long way to the movie theater.

   → It's _____ a long way to the movie theater.

Station 2: Native Americans in the Northwest

people ['piːpl]	Volk
salmon ['sæmən], **salmon** ['sæmən] *(pl)*	Lachs
to **go** *(+ adj)* [gəʊ]	werden
leader ['liːdə]	Führer/-in; Anführer/-in
downriver [ˌdaʊn'rɪvə]	flussabwärts; stromabwärts
cause [kɔːz]	Grund; Ursache
mouth [maʊθ]	Mündung
whale [weɪl]	Wal
to **paddle** ['pædl]	paddeln
canoe [kə'nuː]	Kanu
medicine people ['medsn ˌpiːpl]	Medizinmänner
support *(no pl)* [sə'pɔːt]	Unterstützung; Hilfe
spiritual ['spɪrɪtjuəl]	spirituell; geistig
to **appear** [ə'pɪə]	auftauchen; erscheinen
salmon run ['sæmən ˌrʌn]	Lachswanderung
peaceful ['piːsfl]	friedlich
ceremony ['serɪməni]	Zeremonie
sacred ['seɪkrɪd]	heilig
symbolic [sɪm'bɒlɪk]	symbolisch
to **rise** [raɪz], **rose** [rəʊz], **risen** ['rɪzn]	aufgehen *(Sonne)*
drum [drʌm]	Trommel
raft [rɑːft]	Floß
the gods *(liter)* [ðə 'gɒdz]	die Götter *(literarisch)*
dam [dæm]	Damm; Staumauer
power [paʊə]	Strom; Elektrizität; Energie
timber ['tɪmbə]	Holz; Bauholz
to **remove** [rɪ'muːv]	entfernen; abreißen

outside world ['aʊtsaɪd ˌwɜːld]	Außenwelt
Everything will have changed. [ˌevriθɪŋ wɪl hæv 'tʃeɪndʒd]	Alles wird sich geändert haben.
architecture ['ɑːkɪtektʃə]	Architektur
artwork ['ɑːtwɜːk]	Illustrationen; Bebilderung
longhouse ['lɒŋhaʊs]	Langhaus
totem pole ['təʊtəm ˌpəʊl]	Totempfahl
in favor (of) *(AE)* [ɪn 'feɪvərˌəv]	(da)für; zugunsten (von)
advantage [ədˈvɑːntɪdʒ]	Vorteil
overall [ˌəʊvrˈɔːl]	insgesamt
view [vjuː]	Ansicht; Einstellung; Standpunkt
community [kəˈmjuːnəti]	Gemeinde; Gemeinschaft
disadvantage [ˌdɪsədˈvɑːntɪdʒ]	Nachteil
to **destroy** [dɪˈstrɔɪ]	zerstören
what's more [ˌwɒts ˈmɔː]	außerdem; überdies
deal [diːl]	Handel; Geschäft

4 Synonyms

Write down a word with the same or a similar meaning.

1. wood ⌒ _____

2. go up ⌒ _____

3. energy ⌒ _____

4. boss ⌒ _____

5. reason ⌒ _____

6. take away ⌒ _____

7. be there suddenly ⌒ _____

5 Odd sound out

Cross out the word with the sound that doesn't fit.

1. [iː] people | leader | spiritual | peaceful
2. [æ] paddle | salmon | dam | sacred
3. [ɪ] deal | timber | remove | destroy
4. [eɪ] whale | second | sacred | major
5. [ɑː] rubber | artwork | architecture | calm

6 An important day for Koi

Draw lines to match the sentence parts.

1. The tribe chose Koi　　　　a) to the gods.
2. They put the huge salmon　b) removed at last.
3. Everyone prayed　　　　　c) onto a wooden raft.
4. Koi said that he felt　　　　d) been successful.
5. Their protest had　　　　　e) to carry the symbolic salmon.
6. The dam had been　　　　f) proud of his people.

Skills: How to argue a point in conversation

to **argue** ['ɑːgjuː]	erörtern
eruption [ɪ'rʌpʃn]	Ausbruch *(Vulkan)*
nearby [ˌnɪə'baɪ]	in der Nähe
to **over-exaggerate** [ˌəʊvərɪg'zædʒreɪt]	völlig übertreiben
to **see the bigger picture** [ˌsiː ðə ˌbɪgə 'pɪktʃə]	über den Tellerrand hinausschauen
based on ['beɪst ˌɒn]	basierend auf; beruhend auf
debate [dɪ'beɪt]	Debatte
move [muːv]	Umzug

7 Argue a point!

Complete the dialogue with the correct phrases.

| you've got a point but | unless you can really convince me |
| you're over-exaggerating | decisions based on your feelings |

Erik: Let's go climbing at the weekend!

Mom: No, that's much too dangerous!

Erik: Mom, don't you think _____ ?

Haley: Sure, _____ there are ropes that hold you.

Mom: I'm not going to change my mind _____ !

Erik: Mom, don't make _____ …

Story: The Absolutely True Diary of a Part-Time Indian

junior ['dʒu:niə]	Junior; der/die Jüngere
loser ['lu:zə]	Verlierer/-in; Loser/-in
black eye [blæk ˌaɪ]	blaues Auge
punch [pʌnʃ]	Faustschlag; Boxhieb
to **surround** [sə'raʊnd]	umgeben; umringen
skin [skɪn]	Haut; Fell
gift [gɪft]	Geschenk; Gabe
racist ['reɪsɪst]	rassistisch; Rassist/-in
college ['kɒlɪdʒ]	Universität *(in den USA)*
to **struggle** ['strʌgl]	kämpfen; Mühe haben; ringen
gas(oline) *(AE)* ['gæsli:n]	Benzin
highway *(AE)* ['haɪweɪ]	Landstraße; Bundesautobahn *(amerik.)*; Highway
It wouldn't do me any good. [ˌɪt wʊdnt ˌdu: mi: eni 'gʊd]	Es würde mir nichts nützen.
to **go bad** [ˌgəʊ 'bæd]	schiefgehen; schlecht werden; verderben
strategy ['strætədʒi]	Strategie
struggle ['strʌgl]	Anstrengung; Kampf
soda pop *(AE)* ['səʊdə ˌpɒp]	Limo
imaginary [ɪ'mædʒɪnri]	erfunden; eingebildet
illness ['ɪlnəs]	Krankheit
suit [su:t]	Anzug; Kostüm
to **make fun of** [ˌmeɪk 'fʌn ˌəv]	sich lustig machen über
lame [leɪm]	lahm; langweilig
to **punch** [pʌnʃ]	mit der Faust schlagen; boxen
brain-dead ['breɪnˌded]	hirntot
superhero ['su:pəˌhɪərəʊ]	Superheld
justice ['dʒʌstɪs]	Gerechtigkeit
traitor ['treɪtə]	Verräter/-in

constant [ˈkɒnstənt]	ständig; konstant; stetig; gleichmäßig
to **toss out** [ˌtɒsˈaʊt]	ausstoßen; hinauswerfen
unique [juːˈniːk]	einzigartig

8 Mixed bag: AE words

Put in the correct words.

1. My mom says that _____ is bad for my teeth, so I'm not allowed to drink it. But it's so nice!

2. I was driving on the _____ when I realized that I didn't have enough _____. So I quickly drove to the gas station.

3. Can you take the _____ out, please? I need to cook dinner.

4. I don't have money to go to the movies. I have to wait until my parents give me my _____.

9 Find the missing word

Put in the missing words.

1. tree – oak   fish   – _____
2. nation – president   tribe   – _____
3. peace – peaceful   symbol   – _____
4. valley – mountain   advantage – _____

10 Positive or negative?

Write the words in the correct part of the grid.

justice | loser | black eye | happiness | gift
go bad | illness | lame | advantage | in favor of

Positive	Negative

4

1 Odd word out

Cross out the word that doesn't fit.

1. medicine people | paddleboard | longhouse | totem pole
2. canoe | raft | boat | bike
3. gift | deal | business | corporation
4. fight | superhero | skin | justice
5. constant | debate | unique | brain-dead

2 A crossword: Native Americans

Put in the correct words and find the solution.

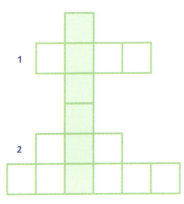

1. Koi's tribe put the salmon on a wooden … .
2. Arnold doesn't say 'reservation' but '…'.
3. Many Native Americans call themselves …s.

Solution:

For Koi's tribe the Elwha River is _____ .

4

Action USA! A trip to die for?

It's to die for! [ˌɪts tə ˈdaɪ fɔː]	Dafür könnte ich sterben!; Das ist unwiderstehlich!
suspicious [səˈspɪʃəs]	verdächtig
misunderstanding [ˌmɪsʌndəˈstændɪŋ]	Missverständnis

13 What's that in AE?

Write down the AE words for the BE words.

1. pocket money – _____
2. petrol – _____
3. motorway – _____
4. queue – _____
5. timetable – _____

14 Check on your … word groups in *Green Line 4*

Think about examples for the word groups in Green Line 4.

1. Kids and school in the US: _____

2. City vs. country life: _____

3. American history: _____

Across cultures 1

1 Contrasts in the US
1. urban, rural   2. wealthy, poor   3. densely, sparsely

2 Word groups: Rural or urban?
In the city: crowded, parks, taxi, skyscraper, Broadway plays, densely populated, noisy
In the country: endless, corn, scenery, wheat, redwood tree, cactus, tractor

3 That's the US!
European, cultural, awesome, extreme, harsh, rural

Unit 1

1 Word friends: American everyday life
1. middle school   2. high school   3. dress code
4. hall pass   5. front yard   6. shopping mall

2 What word?
1. impression   2. hallway   3. restroom   4. suburb

3 Say it in American English!
1. soccer   2. movie   3. store   4. movie theater

4 My new life in the US
downtown, floor, elevator, Luckily, afraid, movie theater, keep in touch

5 Sophie calls Matt
in the middle of nowhere, find, way around, 'm / am tired of, get used to, 'm / am crazy about, No wonder

6 Odd word out
1. curfew   2. give thanks   3. floor   4. foreground
5. be crazy about

7 Matt's dilemma
1. period, 8th-graders   2. geeks, child labor
3. shoppers, rights, prefers

8 Adjectives for people and things

People can be: amazed, dizzy, scared, confident
Things can be: obvious, believable, unrealistic, exaggerated

9 Definitions

1. obvious 2. nightmare 3. escape 4. twice

10 Word friends

1. c) 2. d) 3. e) 4. b) 5. a)

11 Jumbled sentences

1. I'm going to stay right next to you.
2. Lena started to feel sick and dizzy / dizzy and sick.
3. She could easily imagine spending a night in prison.
4. She turned around and came face to face with Matt.

12 Opposites

1. individual 2. boyfriend 3. foreground 4. to dislike

13 Yearbook texts

content, informative, ironic, poses, overdo

14 Check on your ... AE vocabulary

front yard, middle school, high school, restroom, movie, store, downtown, elevator, movie theater, soccer, 8th-grader, period, child labor

Text smart 1

1 Phrasal verbs

a) 1. meet up 2. win over 3. rely on 4. fall for
   5. clean out 6. give away

b) win, over, give away, fall for, clean out, meet up, rely on

2 Word search: Advertising

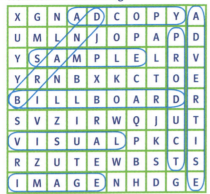

1. billboard 2. sample 3. brand

3 Verb into noun
1. product, production 2. temptation 3. wish 4. advertiser, advertisement, advertising 5. arrival 6. survivor

4 Check on your … adjectives
Lösungsvorschlag:
brand-new, glamorous, lovely, fabulous, great, super, amazing, awesome

Across Cultures 2

1 Talking in English
1. You'd better do your homework!
2. If I were you, I would tell my parents and promise to study more for the next test.
3. I can't see the point of talking to him / her.

2 A crossword: School words

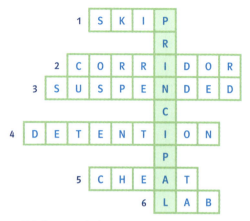

Solution: principal

Unit 2

1 Word friends: New York
1. melting   2. jungle   3. district

2 Definitions
1. intersection   2. a pocketful of   3. inspires   4. melting pot
5. jungle

3 Find the missing word
1. subway   2. artist   3. districts   4. diner

4 In New York
shoestring, diner, truck, cart, fried, pastry, ethnic, combinations

5 What can you say?
1. It's great you've taken the day off.
2. Where's the Empire State Building located?
3. I've read that Bedloe Island is now known as 'Liberty Island'.
4. The food is really delicious. We've saved the best for last!

6 Money, money, money
1. bill, change 2. tip 3. pocket money 4. currencies

7 Bye bye, Lea!
lifted, got in, has come true, perform, complain, shop, gasped, will inspire

8 Say it in a different way
1. speed 2. lead-in 3. laid

9 Graphic novels
panels, shapes, captions, overlap, sequence, long, medium, effects

10 Synonyms
1. panel 2. to perform 3. to shop

11 Word families: Questions and answers
1. unexpected 2. follow-up 3. talk 4. style

12 Phrases for interviews
1. This is a beautiful office. / Where did you grow up?
2. Can you tell me more about …? / Can you explain that to me?
3. How many …? / When did you …?
4. What do you think about …? / What are your goals?
5. Thanks, I enjoyed talking to you. / Thank you for this interesting talk.

13 Check on your … AE spelling
to symbolize, theater, labor, flavor, specialty, to realize, to practice, traveling, center, neighborhood

Text smart 2

1 Internet vocabulary
1. f) 2. e) 3. a) 4. b) 5. d) 6. c)

2 Odd word out
1. machine 2. sequence 3. panel 4. effect 5. talk 6. shape 7. media 8. path

Solutions

3 What do they do?
1. engineer 2. president 3. scientist 4. advertiser
5. reporter

4 Wiki text vs. blog post
Wiki text: factual, informative, reliable, believable
Blog post: entertaining, plays a trick on somebody, questions somebody's motivations, stages a hoax

5 Opposites
1. impossible 2. entertaining / interesting 3. ugly 4. human

6 Make new words
1. undeveloped 2. dishonest 3. impossible 4. lucky
5. insecure 6. unrealistic 7. unexpected 8. healthy
9. useless 10. endless

7 An online rating
space, special effects, Well-developed, believable, breathtaking, weak

8 Check on your ... science vocabulary
moon landing, science, astronaut, engineer, tech, space, space program; **Green Line 3**: invention, discovery, to clone, scientist, to invent, penicillin, steam engine

Across cultures 3

1 Which register?
1. I'm sorry
2. it sucks
3. It was, like, so totally not my thing
4. I don't go there anymore
5. It's so wild to see you again

2 Pronunciation: AE or BE?
1. news, AE 2. dog, BE 3. know, AE 4. bath, BE
5. work, AE 6. ask, AE

3 Where are they from?
1. Canadian 2. German 3. French 4. US / American 5. British

Unit 3

1 Odd word out
1. army 2. pass 3. declare 4. divided

2 American history words
nation, innovation, innovative, to colonize, settlement, eastern, to declare, army, general, settler, united, to descend from, covered wagon

3 European settlement in America
colonized, settlers, belongings, especially, Transportation, traditional, innovation, history

4 Health words
1. medical, examination, caught, infection 2. sick
3. cough, fever

5 Word search: Statistics words

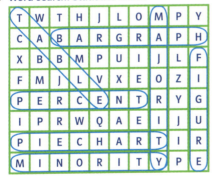

1. table 2. bar graph 3. percent 4. figure

6 Migration words
Nouns: pioneer, mass migration, risk, rider
Verbs: expand, migrate, colonize, risk
Adjectives: wanted, western, colonial, eastern

7 Opposites
1. grandmother 2. majority 3. conclusion 4. calm
5. informal

Solutions

8 Word families: Nouns and adjectives
importance, colonial, medical, nation, history, entertaining

9 Word friends
1. b) 2. d) 3. a) 4. e) 5. f) 6. c)

10 A journey into the unknown: Verbs
comes up to, keep, heads, farm, pack, has abandoned, wonder, owned

11 Jumbled sentences
1. I wonder why rich folks were out here on the trail.
2. It's raining too hard to drive the wagons through the mud.
3. I think you should continue writing Abbie's diary.

12 Check on your ... history vocabulary
lady-in-waiting, quill, slave, reign, crown, Celt, battle, favourite, Victorian, (golden) age, monarch, Tudors, lord, Norman, tribe, empire, emperor, to reign, to invade, to attack, to capture, to marry, to found, to grow up, to burn down, to rebuild, BC, AD

Text smart 3

1 Phrases
1. scared me to death   2. met my expectations   3. be aware of
4. start all over again   5. caught an infection

2 Word friends: Montana
1. b) 2. c) 3. d) 4. e) 5. a)

3 A mind map: On the road
Lösungsvorschlag für Wörter: car, bus, truck, bike, snow tires, to hitchhike, hitchhiking, to get a ride, hitchhiker, cardboard, to stick out, backseat, passenger seat, seat belt, to run over, to drop sb off, to pick sb up

Anordnung der Wörter: *Individuelle Lösung*

4 Check on your … travel words
Transportation: to hitchhike, hitchhiking, to get a ride, truck, hitchhiker, parking lot, backseat, passenger seat, seat belt, to run over, to drop sb off, snow tire
Nature: snow-capped, summit, glacial, valley, wooded, to hunt, grizzly bear, elk, bighorn sheep

Across cultures 4

1 Find the verbs: Household chores
1. load 2. empty, vacuum 3. take, out 4. set

2 Jumbled words: At home
1. household 2. dishes 3. vacuum 4. chore

Unit 4

1 Definitions
1. cougar 2. employee 3. native 4. waterfront 5. orca
6. The outdoors 7. boomtown

2 Different situations
1. You've got no soul! 2. Be true to yourself! 3. I'm in a hurry!

3 Say it in a different way
1. part-time 2. It's my treat 3. major 4. buy time
5. in a hurry 6. kind of

4 Synonyms
1. timber 2. rise 3. power 4. leader 5. cause 6. remove
7. appear

5 Odd sound out
1. spiritual 2. sacred 3. deal 4. second 5. rubber

6 An important day for Koi
1. e) 2. c) 3. a) 4. f) 5. d) 6. b)

7 Argue a point!
you're over-exaggerating, you've got a point but, unless you can really convince me, decisions based on your feelings

8 Mixed bag: AE words
1. soda pop 2. highway, gas(oline) 3. garbage 4. allowance

9 Find the missing word
1. salmon 2. leader 3. symbolic 4. disadvantage

10 Positive or negative?
Positive: justice, happiness, gift, advantage, in favor of
Negative: loser, black eye, go bad, illness, lame

11 Odd word out
1. paddleboard 2. bike 3. gift 4. skin 5. debate

12 A crossword: Native Americans

		S			
1	R	A	F	T	
		C			
		R			
2		R	E	Z	
3	I	N	D	I	A	N

Solution: sacred

13 What's that in AE?
1. allowance 2. gas(oline) 3. highway 4. line 5. schedule

14 Check on your ... word groups in *Green Line 4*
Lösungsvorschlag:
1. **Kids and school in the US:** corridor, gym, lab, to skip, to cheat, to get caught, principal, to be suspended, detention, lunchtime, cheat sheet
2. **City vs. country life:** rural, urban, endless, sparsely populated, densely populated, tractor, skyscraper, scenery, corn, wheat
3. **American history:** immigrant, to colonize, settlement, to declare, army, general, settler, united, to descend from, mass migration, to expand, Native Americans, to suffer from, leader, medicine people, spiritual, sacred, ceremony, totem pole